HOW TO LOOK AT ART

Using Shadows
in art

Joy Richardson

Gareth Stevens Publishing
MILWAUKEE

For a free color catalog describing Gareth Stevens' list of high-quality books and multimedia programs, call 1-800-542-2595 (USA) or 1-800-461-9120 (Canada). Gareth Stevens Publishing's Fax: (414) 225-0377.

Gareth Stevens Publishing would like to thank Gundega Spons of the Milwaukee Art Museum for her kind and professional help with the information in this book.

Library of Congress Cataloging-in-Publication Data available upon request from publisher.
Fax (414) 225-0377 for the attention of the Publishing Records Department.

ISBN 0-8368-2625-6

This North American edition first published in 2000 by
Gareth Stevens Publishing
1555 North RiverCenter Drive, Suite 201
Milwaukee, Wisconsin 53212 USA

Original edition © 1997 by Franklin Watts. First published in 1997 as *Light and Dark* by Franklin Watts, 96 Leonard Street, London, EC2A 4RH, United Kingdom. This U.S. edition © 2000 by Gareth Stevens, Inc. Additional end matter © 2000 by Gareth Stevens, Inc.

Gareth Stevens Editor: Monica Rausch
Gareth Stevens Cover Designer: Joel Bucaro
U.K. Editor: Sarah Ridley
U.K. Designer: Louise Thomas
U.K. Art Director: Robert Walster

Photographs: Reproduced by courtesy of the Trustees of the National Gallery, London ter Brugghen/The Concert pp. 6-7, 26 (detail), Geertgen/The Nativity pp. 4-5, Claude/A Seaport pp. 8-9, Wright/Experiment with the Air Pump pp. 12-13, 29 (detail), Pissarro/Paris, the Boulevard Montmartre pp. 16-17, Monet/The Beach at Trouville pp. 22-23, 29 (detail); reproduced by courtesy of the Prado Museum, Madrid Fortuny/Landscape with a Human Figure pp. 20-21; © photo RMN/Vermeer/The Lacemaker pp. 10-11, 28 (detail); © Tate Gallery, London Turner/Norham Castle, Sunrise pp. 14-15, Whistler/Nocturne in Blue and Gold: Old Battersea Bridge pp. 18-19, Paula Rego/The Dance cover, pp. 24-25, 27 (detail).

Printed in Mexico

1 2 3 4 5 6 7 8 9 04 03 02 01 00

Contents

For additional information about the artists and paintings, see pages 30-31.

The Nativity, at Night
painted by Geertgen tot Sint Jans

Light pierces the dark night as
Jesus is born in a stable.

Can you find nine pairs
of eyes fixed on the baby?

What is watching
in the shadows?

Can you see . . .

a shining angel,

bonfire light,

and holy light from the baby?

The Concert
painted by Hendrick ter Brugghen

Flickering flames make patterns
of light and shadows in the darkness.

Look carefully to see where light from
the lamp and the candle reaches.

This face stands
out, spotlighted
in the darkness.

Shadows fall in the
folds of the clothes.

Light frames the grapes
and makes them look real.

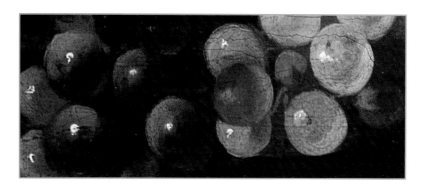

A Seaport
painted by Claude Lorrain

The evening sun sinks in the
sky, casting a glow across the harbor.

The ship looks black against the sun.

Light shimmers across the water.

The setting sun makes long shadows.

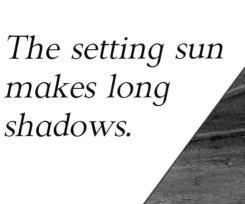

The stone turns golden pink. Can you see what time it is?

The Lacemaker
painted by Jan Vermeer

The lacemaker needs light from
a window to see what she is doing.

Light shows the shape of the work box . . .

and the curves of her face.

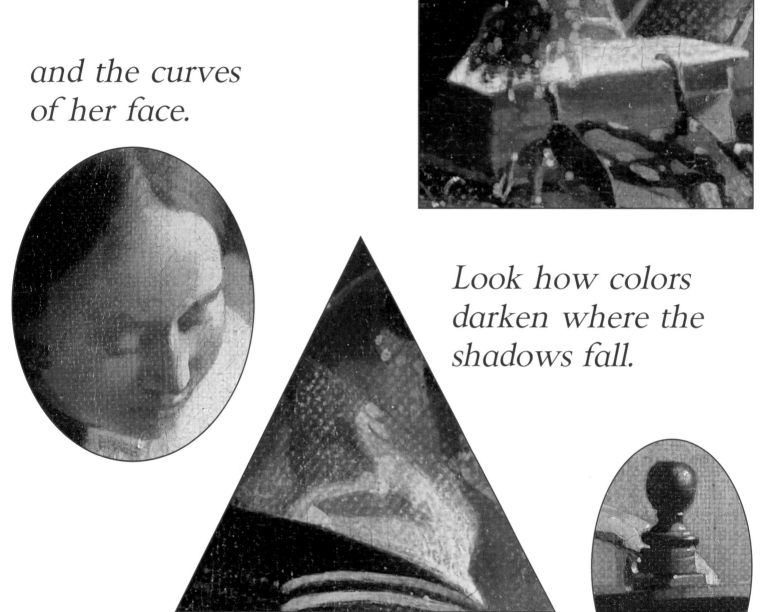

Look how colors darken where the shadows fall.

From which direction is the light coming?

Experiment on a Bird
in the Air Pump
painted by Joseph Wright

Light spotlights the people
watching this experiment with a bird.

Who is curious?
Who is thoughtful?
Who can't bear to look?

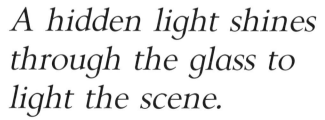

A hidden light shines
through the glass to
light the scene.

The moon breaks
through the clouds.

Norham Castle, Sunrise
painted by J. M. W. Turner

The rising sun fills the air with
light on a fresh, new day.

The sun's brightness fades
the sky to the palest blue.

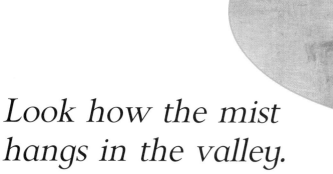

Look how the mist
hangs in the valley.

The hazy castle stands
out like a bruise.

Animals come to
the shining water.

Paris, the Boulevard Montmartre at Night
painted by Camille Pissarro

The artist paints a dark, wet night,
looking down a busy street.

People lose their color in the dark.

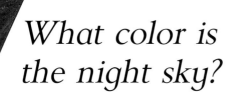

What color is the night sky?

Shop lights,

street lights,

and carriage lights brighten up the night.

The wet pavement reflects the light.

Nocturne: Blue and Gold – Old Battersea Bridge

painted by James Whistler

Night creeps over the misty river,
turning everything blue.

Sparks from fireworks spatter the sky.

Buildings merge with
their reflections.

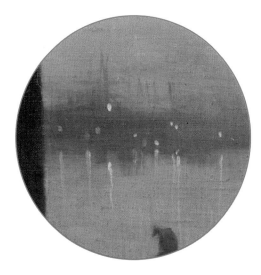

Water and
sky melt into
each other.

Shadowy people cross the bridge.

Landscape with a Human Figure

painted by Mariano Fortuny

The garden shimmers in the light
while a dog naps in the shade.

Strong light can make colors brighter

and shadows deeper.

*The dog lies almost
hidden in the shade.*

*Look how light and shade
color the pebbles on the path.*

The Beach at Trouville
painted by Claude Monet

Between the clouds, the midday sun
shines brightly on the beach.

The dress glares white in the sunlight.

Look at the light on the parasol and the shadow underneath.

Light shines through the moving clouds.

The faces are shaded from the light.

The Dance
painted by Paula Rego

People young and old
dance by the light of the moon.

Moonlight spills
across the sea . . .

and edges Earth
with silver.

Look at the
colors in the
inky-blue sky.

The whirling dancers
cast long shadows.
Whose shadow is this?

Lighting Effects

Lighting colors

Colors need light to
make them brighter.

*Roll a piece of paper to make
a tube. Look through it as you
bring it down to touch your
sleeve, a patch of cloth, a table,
or a book cover. Watch the
colors grow dim and darken.*

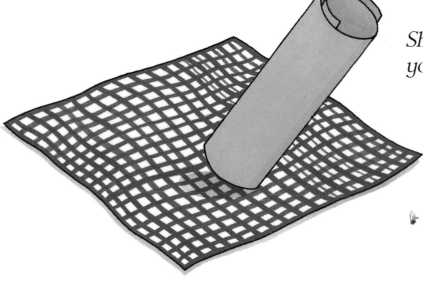

*Shine a flashlight on objects around
you and watch the colors brighten.*

For help, look back
at pages 6, 10, and 20.

Shadow play

Look outside at the shadows falling on the ground. Are they soft or sharp? Look inside at the shadows falling on the floor. Compare them to the shadows you see outside.

Try painting a shadow, showing the surface on which it falls.

For help, look back at pages 8, 20, and 24.

Shaped by light

Light and shadows on curves and corners show how things are shaped.

Place a box or drop a piece of cloth on a table near a window. Look carefully and paint the box or cloth to show where the light and shadows fall. Try adding white or a little black to make the color lighter or darker.

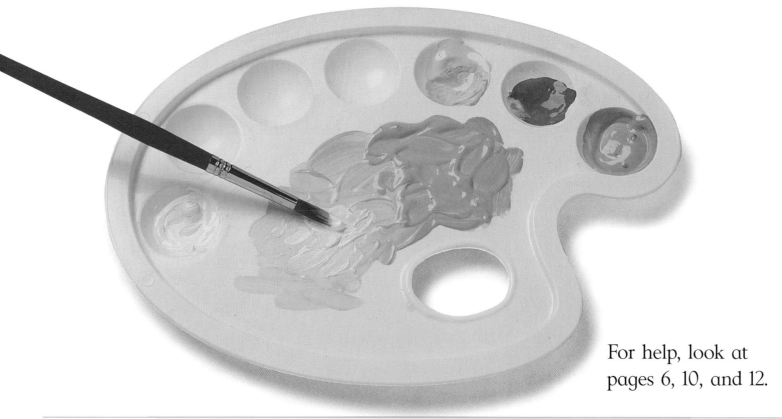

For help, look at pages 6, 10, and 12.

Sky light

Sky colors change with the weather and the time of day.

Look closely at the sky. Try painting a small patch of it.

For help, look at pages 8, 14, 16, 22, and 24.

Faces in the dark

A flashlight or a candle flame lights the darkness in patches and leaves deep shadows.

Darken the room as much as possible. Use a flashlight to light a friend's face from one direction. Try painting the effect this makes.

For help, look back at pages 4, 6, and 12.

More about the paintings in this book

■ The Nativity, at Night *(page 4)*

Geertgen tot Sint Jans (about 1455-1495) worked in Holland making religious paintings for the monastery of the Brethren of St. John. In this painting of Jesus' birth, the main source of light is the baby. This refers to a story of the holy child shining brighter than any earthly light.

■ The Concert *(page 6)*

Hendrick ter Brugghen (about 1588-1629) was Dutch. He learned the dramatic use of lighting, with pools of light set off against deep shadows, from the Italian artist Caravaggio. Ter Brugghen also learned to use light to make details, such as the grapes, look real and natural.

■ A Seaport *(page 8)*

Claude Lorrain (1600-1682) was French but went to live in Italy. Lorrain looked closely at nature, but he also used his imagination to construct beautiful views. People especially admired the way he showed light filling the atmosphere. No one had ever painted the full effect of the sun like this before.

■ The Lacemaker *(page 10)*

Jan Vermeer (1632-1675) was a Dutch painter. He liked to take simple scenes of indoor work or leisure, softly lit by daylight from a window, and paint them to perfection. His pictures are usually small, and he did not paint very many. This painting is only 8.3 inches x 9.4 inches (21 centimeters x 24 centimeters).

■ Experiment on a Bird in the Air Pump *(page 12)*

Joseph Wright (1734-1797) was famous for his lighting effects. He worked out a system with screens so that he could sit in normal light while painting a candlelit scene. In this dramatic picture, a traveling scientist shows how air can be pumped out of the glass bowl and let back in just in time to save the breathless dove.

Norham Castle, Sunrise (page 14)

Joseph Mallord William Turner (1775-1851) was fascinated by the effects of light and weather in the atmosphere. He often painted at Norham Castle on the River Tweed between England and Scotland, and this oil sketch was made there toward the end of his life.

Paris, the Boulevard Montmartre at Night (page 16)

Camille Pissarro (1830-1903) was a good friend of other impressionist painters such as Monet. He liked painting scenes that looked down a road, but this is his only nighttime painting. He painted it from a high window at the end of the street.

Nocturne: Blue and Gold – Old Battersea Bridge (page 18)

James Whistler (1834-1903) was born in America. He painted a series of nocturnes to celebrate the beauty of the night. He said, "The evening mist clothes the riverside with poetry, like a veil; ... fairyland is before us." His work had a mixed reception at first. The art critic Ruskin accused him of "flinging a pot of paint in the public's face."

Landscape with a Human Figure (page 20)

Mariano Fortuny (1838-1874) died young, but before he died, he was already recognized as the best painter of his time in Spain. As a young man, he spent a few years in Morocco, and there he became familiar with the challenge of painting in very bright light.

The Beach at Trouville (page 22)

Claude Monet (1840-1926) made this painting in July 1870 during a seaside holiday with his new wife, Camille (on the left in the picture), and friends. Monet painted the picture on the beach. Grains of sand are still stuck in the paint.

The Dance (page 24)

Paula Rego (born in 1935) grew up in Portugal, where this painting is set. The painting draws strongly on memories of childhood, growing up, and marriage. The daughter, mother, and grandmother in the background stand for the three ages of woman, and the whole painting represents the dance of life.

Glossary

casting: to throw an object or shadow so that it falls upon another object.

fades: loses color or freshness.

flickering: an unsteady light that goes on and off.

frames (v): surrounds, as if in a frame.

glares: reflects a bright, blinding light.

impressionists: painters from the 1870s who believed in painting the first "impression" of their subjects in short dabs of color, conveying reflected light more than a realistic image.

landscape: a setting of natural scenery.

merge: unite to form one object.

nocturne: a work of art dealing with night.

pierces: makes a hole through or makes a way into.

shimmers: reflects or shines with a wavering, flickering light.

spotlighted (v): lit by a strong, projected spot of light.

Web Sites

Global Show-n-Tell Art
www.telenaut.com/gst/

Kidz Draw
www.kidzdraw.com/artist.htm

Due to the dynamic nature of the Internet, some web sites stay current longer than others. To find additional web sites, use a reliable search engine with one or more of the following keywords: *art, impressionism, Claude Monet, painting,* and *Camille Pissarro.*

Index